THE RACCOON

BY
JEROLYN ANN NENTL

EDITED BY
DR. HOWARD SCHROEDER
Professor in Reading and Language Arts
Dept. of Elementary Education
Mankato State University

PRODUCED AND DESIGNED BY
BAKER STREET PRODUCTIONS
Mankato, MN

CRESTWOOD HOUSE
Mankato, Minnesota

LIBRARY OF CONGRESS CATALOGING IN PUBLICATION DATA

Nentl, Jerolyn Ann.
  The raccoon.

  (Wildlife, habits and habitat)
  SUMMARY: Introduces the physical characteristics, habits, and natural environment of the raccoon.
  1. Raccoons--Juvenile literature. (1. Raccoons) I. Schroeder, Howard. II. Title. III. Series: Wildlife, habits & habitat.
QL737.C26N46   1984   599.74'443   83-21072
ISBN 0-89686-246-1 (lib. bdg.)

International Standard Book Number:	Library of Congress Catalog Card Number:
Library Binding 0-89686-246-1	83-21072

ILLUSTRATION CREDITS:

Lynn Rogers: Cover, 43
Nadine Orabona: 4, 8, 11, 15, 30, 37, 38-39
Phil & Loretta Hermann: 7, 12, 17, 27, 34, 41, 42
Jerg Kroener: 18
Leonard Lee Rue III/Tom Stack & Associates: 21, 28
Charles Palek/Tom Stack & Associates: 24-25
Richard P. Smith/Tom Stack & Associates: 33
Cheryl R. Todd: 35
Photo Library: 44

CRESTWOOD HOUSE

Hwy. 66 South, Box 3427
Mankato, MN 56002-3427

TABLE OF CONTENTS

INTRODUCTION:

"Mom, come here! Hurry!"

Debbie's mother rushed to the kitchen when she heard her daughter calling. To her surprise, nothing was wrong when she got there.

"Look," Debbie said, pointing out the sliding glass doors onto the back porch. Her mother peered out into the darkness. There was just enough glow from the kitchen light for her to see a small gray animal with a striped tail go running off into the night.

"It was eating the dog's food!" Debbie said, still very excited at seeing this strange visitor up close. "I came into the kitchen to get something to eat. When I switched on the light, there it was. The animal was picking up Tramp's dry food one piece at a time. It looked like it was washing the pieces in Tramp's water dish before it ate them. The animal's face had a black mask."

A raccoon slips through the night.

4

CHAPTER ONE

An American mammal

What is this animal with the bandit mask and the striped tail? It is the raccoon, one of the best-known, North American animals.

The raccoon is a mammal of medium size, about as large as a small dog. It is quite shy and gentle.

The raccoon is truly an American animal. There are no native raccoons in the Old World of Europe and Asia. The North American Raccoon, which this book is about, lives throughout Canada, the United States and Central America. The only places in North America where it does not live are in parts of the Rocky Mountains and the Great Basin area of California, Utah and Nevada. A similiar raccoon lives in South America. As a rule, the raccoon is found from sea level up to an altitude of around two thousand feet. A few raccoons have even been seen as high as nine thousand feet in some mountain ranges.

From Canada to Panama

In Canada, raccoons are found from Nova Scotia to British Columbia. Most of them live in the southern parts of the provinces, but a few have been found as far north as Wood Buffalo National Park in Alberta, Canada.

In the lower forty-eight states of the United States, raccoons are common from the east coast to the west coast. There have also been reports of raccoons living on two islands off the southeast coast of Alaska. These raccoons were not native to the islands, however. They had been brought there from the lower forty-eight states.

Twenty-nine subspecies, or kinds, of North American Raccoon have been identified by scientists. These differ slightly in size and color. The quality of their fur and their habits differ slightly, too. It depends on how far north or south the raccoons live.

Giant ancestors

The ancestors of the raccoon were huge beasts that roamed North and South America thousands of years ago. Through centuries of development these animals decreased in size. The raccoons range across the two continents, however, remains much the same today as its early ancestors was.

Raccoons are shy animals.

These animals were also the ancestors of today's bears, dogs and weasels. The raccoon is often called "the bear's little brother" because of the shape of its body, its naked-soled feet and the way it walks.

Raccoons, known simply as 'coons to many people, are remarkable wild animals. People have moved into their territory during the last few centuries, but the raccoons have survived. Raccoons are able to live close to humans, with no trouble at all.

Raccoons enjoy water.

CHAPTER TWO:

A heavy-set animal

A raccoon is a heavy-set animal — short and fat. This gives it an appealing, roly-poly appearance. Exactly how big a raccoon is depends on where it lives, the food supply available to it, and the time of year. An adult raccoon may weigh as little as eight pounds (3.6 kg) or as much as twenty pounds (9 kg). Some may reach forty pounds (18 kg). Male raccoons are usually heavier than females. All raccoons are fattest in the fall.

The heaviest weight ever reported for a raccoon is sixty-two pounds (28.3 kg). This was a male raccoon, which was weighed in late fall.

A raccoon has a broad head that tapers sharply into a short, pointed nose. It has a long, round, bushy tail and short, broad ears that stand straight up. An adult raccoon can vary in length from twenty-four to forty inches (600-1000 mm), from the tip of its nose to the tip of its tail. A raccoon's tail is about one-third of its total length. The average height of a raccoon, at the shoulder, is about twelve inches (300 mm).

Long, soft fur

The thick hairy coat of the raccoon, which is sometimes called its pelage, or pelt, is long and soft. It is in two layers: short, fine underfur covered by coarse guard hairs. The underfur keeps the raccoon warm. The guard hairs protect the underfur from wear and tear. These guard hairs are long and loose, giving the raccoon a shaggy appearance. They are so long on some raccoons that they drag on the ground when it walks.

Both male and female raccoons are alike in color. The underfur is gray or brown. The guard hairs are yellowish-brown with black and white tips. Together, they give the raccoon a streaked gray appearance over most of its upper body. Sometimes a raccoon's gray coat will have a brown or a cinnamon-red cast, especially on the back of the neck.

A raccoon's belly is a paler yellowish-brown or gray. It's feet are also yellowish-gray. A raccoon's face is creamy white, with a black stripe or band across its eyes and cheeks. A raccoon looks as if it is wearing a permanent mask!

There is also a small black stripe that goes from the tip of its black nose up between its small, dark eyes to a point between its ears. Raccoons have white whiskers, too.

Four to seven black stripes or bands ring a rac-

The raccoon has a thick layer of fur.

coon's bushy, yellowish-gray tail. These rings are not always too clear on the bottom side of the tail. When curled up to sleep, the rings help the raccoon blend in with its surroundings.

A raccoon molts, or sheds, its hairy coat once each year. This loss of old hair starts on the raccoon's head and slowly proceeds down its whole body to its tail. This process takes several months. It begins in early spring with the first warm weather and is fin-

Raccoons wear a permanent "mask."

ished as summer begins. New fur slowly grows in to replace the old fur that is shed. This growth of new fur lasts throughout the summer.

The new fur is shorter than the old fur. It will grow longer and get thicker as autumn turns into winter. This is called priming. Like molting, priming begins at the raccoon's head. It proceeds across its whole body to its tail. A raccoon's coat reaches its longest and thickest in December and January, when the weather is coldest. This is when a raccoon's coat is said to be in its prime, or best, condition.

Molting and priming are more important to raccoons living in the North. It is nature's way of helping the raccoon stay cool in the summer and warm in the winter. In the South, where the weather is warm throughout the year, molting and priming are not as important.

Strong legs, nimble feet

The hind legs of a raccoon are long and strong. They support most of the weight of its body. The forelegs are shorter than the hind legs. This gives the raccoon its humped-back appearance.

A raccoon has five long, slim toes on each foot. Each toe has a short but sharp, strong claw. The claws are curved and non-retractile, which means raccoons cannot pull their claws back in like cats. The soles, or pads, of a raccoon's feet have no fur, and the heel can easily be seen.

Each hind foot is large and flat, making a foot print two to four-and-a-half inches long (5.1-11.5 cm). It looks much like the footprint of a small child. This is because a raccoon's feet are plantigrade. Plantigrade animals walk on their entire foot, with their heel touching the ground. Other mammals such as dogs or cats walk only on their toes. A raccoon's usual walk is a slow, pigeon-toed waddle. When chased, however, it can run quite fast.

A raccoon's forefeet are smaller than its hind feet. They are very sensitive, like a human's hands. A raccoon has a very gentle, delicate touch.

The toes on a raccoon's forefeet are so flexible that they are often called fingers. Raccoons can use their forefeet almost as well as monkeys can. A raccoon often sits back on its hind legs and uses its forefeet to examine things. It can pick up objects as small as a kernel of corn. It can also open many kinds of things, such as gate latches.

All five of its senses are very well-developed — sight, touch, taste, smell and hearing. The sense of touch is the most developed, especially in its forefeet and the tip of its nose.

Raccoons communicate with many different kinds of sounds that are difficult to describe. Adult raccoons have a shrill wail almost like a whistle. Deep in the woods in the middle of the night, it can sound like the long drawn-out "whoo-oo-oo-oo" of an owl.

Many people consider raccoons to be very intelligent. Scientists believe they can learn about as well as cats, but not as well as monkeys. They can make good pets, especially when they are young. They are playful and like to be held and petted. Raccoons are also quite clever and very curious. Such things can get them into trouble when they get older. Raccoons have been known to open cupboard doors and drawers and take everything out of them. It is usually best, though, not to make a pet out of any wild animal because they often lose the ability to survive on their own.

Its looks and habits make the raccoon a very interesting animal to study. It is an easy animal to identify. No other animal has such a round little body, black face mask, and ringed tail.

You have to keep food locked up tight when a raccoon is around!

CHAPTER THREE:

Do raccoons wash their food?

The raccoon has some of the most interesting habits of any North American animal. Its sleeping habits are a good example. To sleep, a raccoon often lies on its back and covers its eyes with its forefeet. It may also roll itself into a ball, putting the top of its head flat against a tree limb or on the ground between its forelegs.

For many years, it was believed that raccoons always washed their food before eating it. In fact, its scientific name, "lotor," means "the washer." Different reasons were suggested as to why raccoons did this. One was that raccoons were very clean. Another was that raccoons had to wet their food in order to swallow it, since they had no saliva glands to moisten their mouth. Neither is true, however. Raccoons are not any cleaner in their habits than any other wild animal. And they have well-developed saliva glands, which means that raccoons do not have any trouble swallowing dry food.

The truth is that raccoons do not wash their food. Raccoons may dunk their food in water. They may

A raccoon often lies on its back before going to sleep.

even swish it around before they eat it, so it looks like they are washing it. Some scientists believe that raccoons may do this out of boredom. Other scientists believe that it is an instinct raccoons are born with —a memory of how their ancestors got food along the shores of rivers, streams, lakes, and oceans.

This raccoon enjoys a meal at low tide along the coast of British Columbia, Canada.

18

Raccoons like water and trees

Wild raccoons are still most at home near water. The raccoon is not an aquatic animal, or one that lives in water. Yet it spends much of its time wading in shallow water or mud near the water's edge looking for something to eat. A raccoon's naked-soled feet and long toes, plus the short hair at its wrists, make this kind of food foraging easy.

The raccoon is a good swimmer. It does the dog paddle if it wants to cross a body of water. Often the raccoon uses its tail as a rudder, to help it go in the right direction.

Next to water, what raccoons want most is trees. Raccoons are good climbers, and are one of the few mammals that can climb down a tree head-first. They often climb along tree branches with their backs hanging toward the ground. They can do this because of their ability to grasp with their feet. Since a raccoon's feet are not webbed, they can spread their toes. Their sharp claws help them cling to a tree, too. As they grow older and heavier, however, raccoons cannot move about so easily in the trees. Some may even slide down a tree tail first!

Raccoons like to make their homes in the hollows of large trees high above the ground. Here they can sleep, take refuge from predators, and bear their litters of young, called cubs. They are not true "aboreal" animals, however, because they do not always live in trees. Raccoons like to live along streams in farming country and on the prairies, too. They are also found in treeless areas. In these places, raccoons scratch out a home beneath rocky ledges, or in holes and cracks in the banks of streams. Raccoons have been known to live in wood piles, drainpipes, and caves. They have even been found in the attics of houses!

Living alone

Raccoons are solitary animals and live alone. The adults are rarely seen together.

A raccoon does not have just one home, or sleeping site. It may sleep almost anywhere. Some raccoons may change sleeping sites several times a year. Others may change them almost every day. It depends partly on the food supply. The raccoon goes where there is food to eat. A favorite spot may become a more permanent sleeping site. This site may then be called a den. Raccoons will also find a new place to rest when they are disturbed by a human or another animal.

Each raccoon has a home range across which it roams. A raccoon that lives near a city or town may

A hollow in a tree is a favorite home for raccoons.

have a home range as small as twelve acres (5 ha). One that lives on the wide-open prairies may have a range as large as twenty square miles (5,000 ha). Exactly how large a home range the raccoon has depends upon how old it is and how many other raccoons live in the area. It will also depend upon how many people live nearby. In general, the home ranges of male raccoons are larger than those of female raccoons.

A raccoon roams over one small part of its home range at a time. It will change from one area to another, depending on the time of year and the food supply. Some parts of the home range may not be used very much. Others may be used often.

As a rule, a raccoon does not defend its home range like many other animals do. Sometimes home ranges may even overlap. An adult male raccoon, however, may defend a good feeding spot for awhile.

Raccoons eat almost anything

A raccoon is a true "omnivorous" animal, which means it does not stick to either an animal or plant diet. It eats both kinds of food. A raccoon will eat almost anything. Even garbage is high on its list of favorite foods. Raccoons living in the woods check out camp sites and picnic places for any scraps of food that may have been left. Raccoons near farms, towns or cities visit any place where food may have been grown, cooked or stored. Trash piles, garbage cans, and pet food dishes are often raided.

Exactly what a raccoon eats changes with the time of year and the area in which it lives. Raccoons tend to eat more plants than animals. They eat fruits, nuts, and grains. Acorns are their favorite nuts, but they will also eat hickory nuts, beech nuts, pecans and walnuts. Corn is by far their favorite grain. They like it best when it is in its "milk stage." This is when it is green, before it has hardened. Raccoons eat wild berries of all kinds, whenever they can find them. At times, a raccoon may add grasses, weeds, seeds, and flower buds, to its diet.

The animals eaten by raccoons are mostly "invertebrates," or animals that have no backbone. Raccoons favor crayfish, crabs, clams, and oysters that are found in mud or sand. They often swish these foods back and forth in the water to remove the sand and dirt. It may be this habit that gave the raccoon its name and its fame as a food-washer.

When they can catch them, small animals such as squirrels, gophers, and mice are important food for raccoons. They will also eat turtles, turtle eggs, frogs, and fish.

Raccoons can become quite expert at raiding farms and ranches. They like young chickens, tur-

Raccoons love corn!

keys, and ducks. They will take the eggs of these birds, too. Raccoons also eat small birds, pheasants, and quail.

Raccoons use their sense of touch to explore each piece of food they eat. They will turn the piece over and over with their "fingers," and rub it between their forefeet. Scientists have learned that raccoons "feel" their food before eating it, more than they "wash" it.

Active at night

Raccoons are nocturnal animals. This means they are most active at night and sleep during the day. As darkness comes each evening, they begin their daily search for food. They are most active in the darkest hours, around midnight. At times raccoons may also forage during the twilight hours, before sunrise and after sunset. This changes a little with the weather. On very cloudy days, a raccoon may be active during the middle of the day.

Raccoons are not often active in the sunshine, unless they have been disturbed. The exceptions are those raccoons that live near the shores of the oceans. These raccoons will search for food at low tide, even during the day. Raccoons may sometimes be seen on sunny days, however, as they like to sleep sprawled on big limbs high up in a tree.

Raccoons are most active at night.

Mates in the spring

Raccoons mate during the late winter and early spring. The days are beginning to grow longer, and this seems to arouse their instinct to reproduce. A male and female may live together for a few weeks during the mating season. Then they go their separate ways.

After mating, the mother raccoon carries her young within her for about sixty days. This time of development is called the gestation period. The mother raccoon does not build a special nest for her young. A few days before the young are born, she simply chews or scratches together a wood or dirt bed to hold them.

Three or four young, called cubs, are born in late spring. A raccoon cub weighs less than three ounces (85 g) at birth. It is covered with fur, but its eyes and ears are closed. The eyes and ears will not open for several weeks. A raccoon cub must depend upon its mother for everything during this time.

The black mask and rings on a raccoon's tail will

The eyes and ears on these four-day-old raccoons are still closed.

not appear for about two or three weeks. Its guard hairs will not develop until it is about six weeks old. When it is about seven weeks old, it begins its first molt. Once the new fur is in, a cub looks like an adult raccoon. Yet it is still much smaller.

Mother raises the cubs

It is the mother raccoon's job to raise the young cubs. She stays with them during the night after their birth, not even leaving to eat. For the next few nights, she will forage for food only a short distance away. A mother raccoon is very protective of her helpless young cubs. She may become aggressive toward any animal that gets too near her den. If she feels her young have been disturbed too much, she may move them to a new site. She carries them in her mouth, holding them with her teeth so she does not drop them. She grasps each one either at its neck or its middle, and moves them one at a time.

A mother raccoon nurses her young for three or four months. They grow and develop, feeding only on their mother's milk. A mother raccoon sits up on her hind legs to nurse her cubs. She may hold them up to her nipples with her forefeet so they can nurse. Mother raccoons search nightly for food for themselves during this time, but they bring nothing back to their dens for the young ones.

The cubs "purr" quietly when content. If lonely or hungry, they let their mother know with a high-pitched whimper or whine. A mother raccoon also keeps in touch with her cubs with a low, twittering "purr." She warns them of danger with a high-pitched cry.

The young cubs cannot walk until they are at least a month old. Their legs are not strong enough to hold them. Once they are a few months old, they try to follow their mother on her nightly food trips. Most of the time they cannot keep up with her, and must give up and return to the den. The cubs will not

This is a real bundle of mischief!

be strong enough to follow her until they are three or four months old. By then they will be able to run and climb trees. They still may nurse a little, but they also begin to eat food that they find for themselves during these nightly trips. Mother and cubs forage for food together now. They travel farther and farther, as the young ones get stronger. They sleep together wherever they can find shelter.

By the time the cubs are about five months old, they go out on short trips of their own, without their mother. Each may go alone, or they may go in pairs or small groups. By early autumn, the cubs may spend several days and nights away from their mothers. Then they are off to find a home range of their own. Cubs in the Far North may stay with their mother longer, perhaps throughout the winter. This helps them keep warm. All may sleep together, or groups of two or three may find sleeping sites nearby. By the next spring, they, too, are off on their own.

Once they are a year old, the young raccoons are called yearlings. Neither male nor female will reach their full growth until they are two years old.

A winter's sleep

Some people believe that raccoons hibernate for the winter. This is not true. Raccoons in the North will curl up in a favorite tree and go to sleep, when the weather turns cold. They may sleep for as long as four months. They do not eat, drink or rid themselves of any body wastes. This time is called a raccoon's dormant period. It is not a time of true hibernation.

True hibernation requires a decrease in an animal's body temperature and rate of heartbeat. Such a decrease dulls its senses so it cannot awaken until its body is warmed in the spring. A raccoon may sleep for a long time, but its body temperature and heart rate stay about the same as always. This is why this period is not considered by scientists to be a time of true hibernation. Movement or noise nearby can easily awaken raccoons. Then they may forage for something to eat, even if the snow is deep. They also may move to a new sleeping site. A single warm day may rouse raccoons from their deep sleep, too.

A northern raccoon's dormant time lasts from November or December until February, March or April. It depends upon the weather each year. A raccoon may lose fifty per cent of its body weight during this long winter's sleep. To stay alive, it uses the extra fat put on by eating more during the fall.

Raccoons in the South may be active all year. This is true since the weather in the South is warm all year. Yet these raccoons may also curl up at a favorite site to sleep, if the weather turns cool. Southern raccoons may lose fifteen to thirty per cent of their body weight during the winter months.

It's uncommon to see a raccoon that's moving around in winter.

A tough fighter

Many animals prey on the raccoon. Its enemies include wild cats, wolves, coyotes, fishers and foxes. Even owls and alligators try to eat them! These predators seldom kill healthy adult raccoons, however. It is the raccoon cubs or the old and sickly raccoons that are most often the victim of these predators. Healthy adult raccoons are very good at finding places to hide. They are also quite able to defend themselves. They growl, hiss, snarl, and snort. They also make sharp barks, like those of a

A fully-grown raccoon is very capable of defending itself.

Raccoons have strong, sharp teeth.

dog. A raccoon can sound very fierce and may even snap at its enemy.

Raccoons can appear very fierce, too. They may bare their teeth, lay back their ears and swish their tail back and forth. They may arch their back and raise their shoulders and tail. All this makes a raccoon look bigger than it really is. With luck, such a display may scare away the predator. When forced to fight, a raccoon can be very tough. It fights with its strong, sharp claws.

If it decides not to fight, a raccoon will press itself close to the ground and try to back away.

Most raccoons in the wild only live to be about five years old, although a few may live to be twelve or fifteen years old. Most die either of starvation or at the hands of humans. The raccoon is trapped for its valuable fur and hunted for its tasty meat. Many are also hit by motor vehicles.

CHAPTER FOUR:

The long, soft coat of the raccoon is a prized pelt. Its dark flesh is very tasty to many people. Because of this, raccoons have been trapped and hunted for several centuries.

The early pioneers hunted the raccoons for food. They used the skins for caps and coats to keep themselves warm. Almost every man and boy had a 'coon skin cap with the tail dangling in back. This was the style of Daniel Boone's cap.

Raccoon skins were also used as money by the early settlers. There was such a demand for raccoon pelts at one time that the animal became quite scarce. Once the demand for pelts decreased, the raccoons quickly grew again in numbers.

Trapping for pelts

Trappers want a raccoon's pelt when it is prime. This is when it will bring the best price on the fur-trading market. The pelts of northern raccoons have the most value, since they are longer and thicker. Those of southern raccoons have little value.

The soft, warm fur of northern raccoons is prized for making coats and hats.

Raccoons are not trapped in the summer, when their fur is shorter.

Raccoon pelts are used today for coats and for fur trim on other garments. Some raccoon skins are also sheared and dyed to look like mink and fox. Then they are sold as fake furs.

Trappers today can still earn a steady winter income from raccoon pelts. The value of pelts changes, however. The price per pelt was $1-$3 in the middle 1950's. By 1980, it was $20-$30. This increase came because other fur-bearing animals were becoming extinct and their pelts were no longer available. Raccoon pelts were more in demand than ever before.

During the 1930's, less than three hundred thousand raccoon skins were taken a year. By 1980, the number was almost four million per year.

Hunting for meat and sport

The raccoon is still a popular game animal today. In some places raccoons are hunted at night, most often with a special breed of dogs that can pick up the raccoon's scent. A raccoon will run for miles, around trees and across logs and streams. It will zigzag back and forth, with the dogs and hunters chasing it. Finally, it will escape or be treed by the dogs. Once the hunters catch up to the dogs, they shine their flashlights on the raccoon and shoot it. If

A raccoon goes up a tree to escape from hunting dogs.

A treed raccoon.

they cannot take aim at it, they may decide to cut the tree down. A raccoon has been known to cling to a tree even when it is being felled. And if the raccoon survives the fall of the tree, the chase may be on once again.

For those who like a good chase, nothing is better than 'coon hunting in the middle of the night!

The dark flesh of a raccoon is a real treat. It is at its best, sweet and juicy, in the late summer and early fall.

A "masked bandit" soaks up some sun.

The future

Today, the raccoon is one of the few animals that seems to be extending the limits of its range. One reason for this is its regular breeding habits. A second reason is its ability to adapt to humans. Even with hunting and trapping, the raccoon is in no danger of extinction at this time.

The challenge is to maintain this good balance. This must be done, or future generations will not be able to enjoy this animal with the bandit mask, stripped tail, and curious habits — the North American Raccoon.

The outlook for the raccoon is very good.

MAP:

Most raccoons in North America are found within the shaded areas.

INDEX/GLOSSARY:

WILDLIFE
HABITS & HABITAT

READ AND ENJOY THE SERIES:

THE **WHITETAIL** • THE **PHEASANT**

THE **BALD EAGLE** • THE **WOLVES**

THE **SQUIRRELS** • THE **BEAVER**

THE **GRIZZLY** • THE **MALLARD**

THE **RACCOON** • THE **WILD CATS**

THE **RATTLESNAKE** • THE **SHEEP**

THE **ALLIGATOR** • THE **CARIBOU**

THE **CANADA GOOSE** • THE **FOXES**